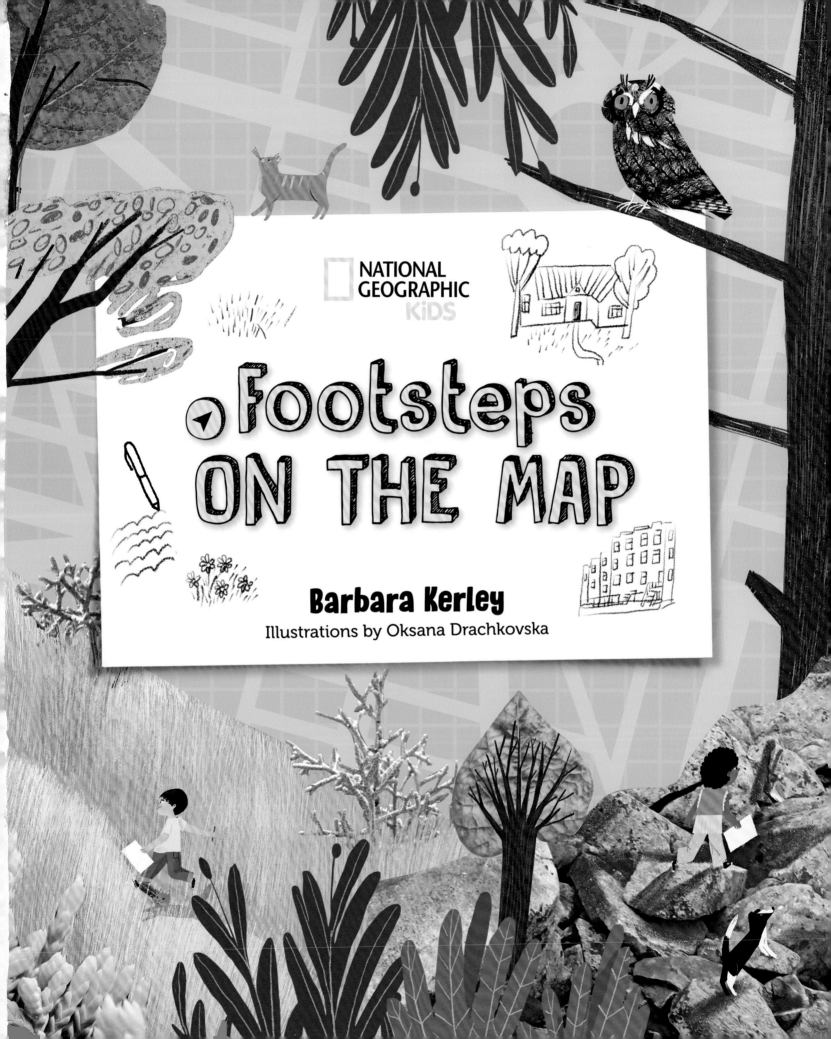

NATIONAL GEOGRAPHIC
KiDS

Footsteps
ON THE MAP

Barbara Kerley

Illustrations by Oksana Drachkovska

Setting out,

pen in hand.

First steps

on the map.

Meadow grass.

Woodland path.

Bird and Leaf.

Moss and fern.

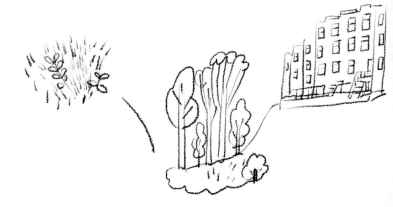

Rushing creek.

Ocean's roar.

Dappled shade.

Forest deep.

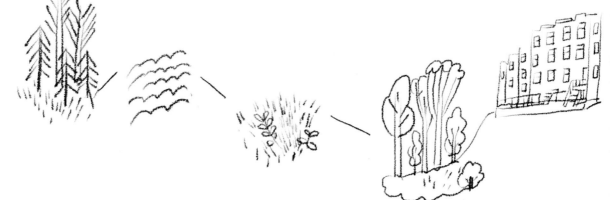

Icy drink

and berry snack.

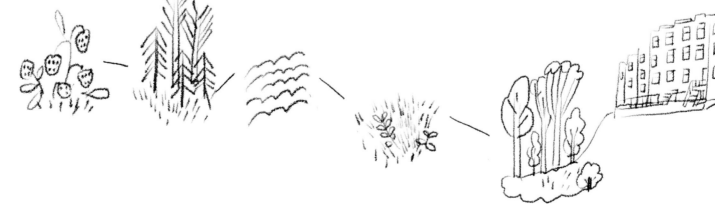

Another step
forward

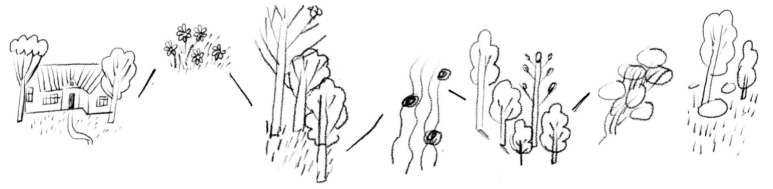

on the map.

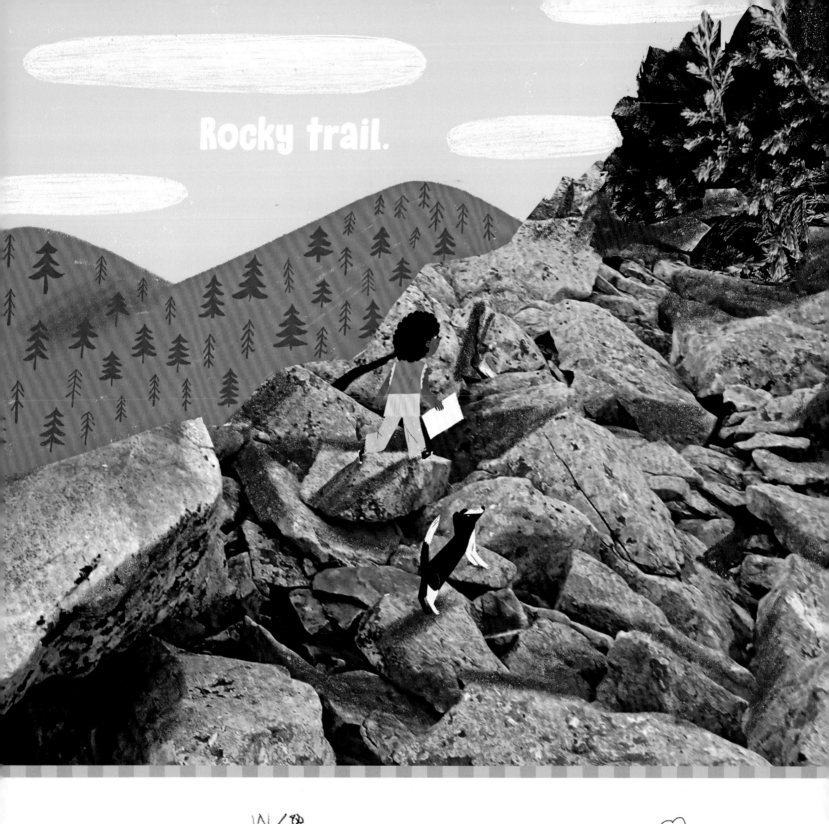

Rocky trail.

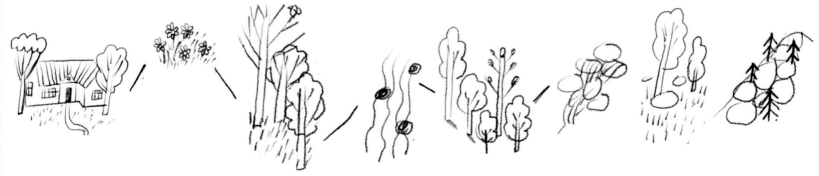

Mountain steep.

Sun and sky.

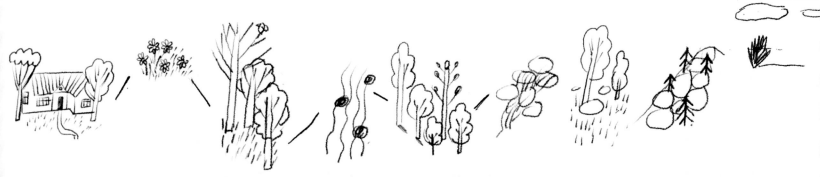

Wind and brush.

Up and up

and up and up!

New friends ...

Where You Are

The kids in this book each make a map of the things they see on their walk. But most maps show an area as if you were up above, looking down at everything all at once. You can make a map like this, too.

Start by mapping your bedroom. You can use small drawings called **symbols** to show where your bed, closet, and window are in the room. Is there a bookcase? A chair? A place to put toys? Add those things, too! You can add **labels** to your map and even cut out pictures to glue or tape onto it.

A map of your bedroom might look something like this:

Now you're ready to make a map of your favorite park! Picture the park in your mind. Are there swings? A slide? Picnic tables? A basketball court? Be sure to include symbols for these things on your map. You can list your symbols in a **map key** to help you keep track of everything in the park.

Here's what a map of a park might look like:

Map Key

 Tree

 Picnic table

 Flowers

 Swing

Sidewalk

Where Do You Want to Go?

Maps are a great way to understand the place where you live. They are also good for learning about places where you haven't been.

Earth is round, but this map shows how it would look if it were spread out flat. Symbols and labels show the locations of mountains, rivers, deserts, forests, oceans, and more.

A **compass rose** shows the **cardinal directions: north, south, east,** and **west.** The directions will help you find your way as you explore. A map of the world will show you that North America is north of South America, Asia is east of Europe, and Antarctica is south of all other land in the world.

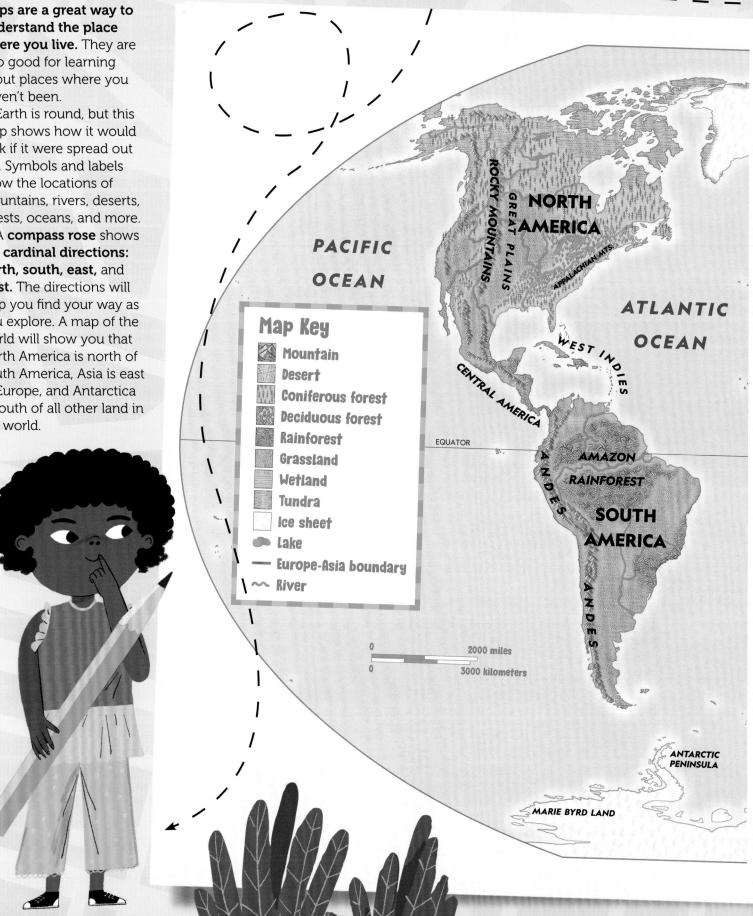

PACIFIC OCEAN

NORTH AMERICA

ROCKY MOUNTAINS

GREAT PLAINS

APPALACHIAN MTS.

ATLANTIC OCEAN

WEST INDIES

CENTRAL AMERICA

EQUATOR

ANDES

AMAZON RAINFOREST

SOUTH AMERICA

ANDES

ANTARCTIC PENINSULA

MARIE BYRD LAND

Map Key

- Mountain
- Desert
- Coniferous forest
- Deciduous forest
- Rainforest
- Grassland
- Wetland
- Tundra
- Ice sheet
- Lake
- Europe-Asia boundary
- ～ River

| 0 | 2000 miles |
| 0 | 3000 kilometers |

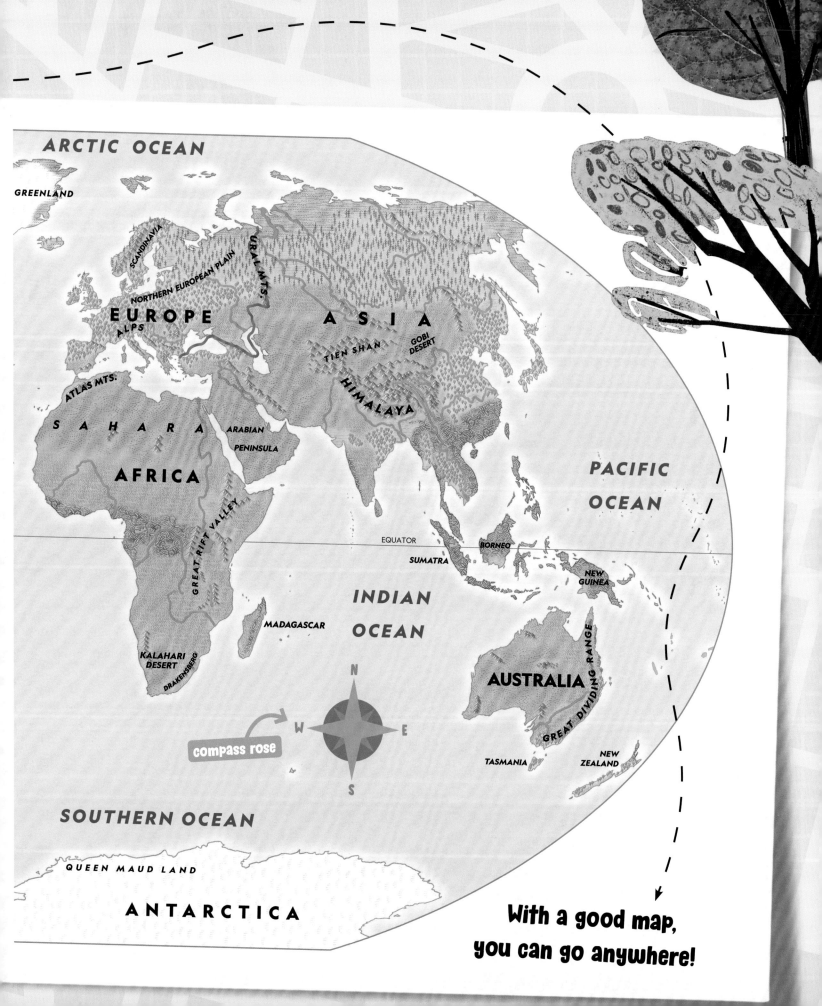

ARCTIC OCEAN

GREENLAND

SCANDINAVIA

NORTHERN EUROPEAN PLAIN

URAL MTS.

EUROPE
ALPS

ASIA

TIEN SHAN

GOBI DESERT

HIMALAYA

ATLAS MTS.

S A H A R A

ARABIAN PENINSULA

AFRICA

PACIFIC OCEAN

GREAT RIFT VALLEY

EQUATOR

BORNEO

SUMATRA

NEW GUINEA

INDIAN OCEAN

MADAGASCAR

KALAHARI DESERT

DRAKENSBERG

AUSTRALIA

GREAT DIVIDING RANGE

N
W   E
S

compass rose

TASMANIA

NEW ZEALAND

SOUTHERN OCEAN

QUEEN MAUD LAND

ANTARCTICA

With a good map, you can go anywhere!

FOR MARFÉ FERGUSON DELANO AND ERICA GREEN —BK
FOR MY FATHER —OD

Published by National Geographic Partners, LLC.

Since 1888, the National Geographic Society has funded more than 14,000 research, conservation, education, and storytelling projects around the world. National Geographic Partners distributes a portion of the funds it receives from your purchase to National Geographic Society to support programs including the conservation of animals and their habitats. To learn more, visit natgeo.com/info.

For more information, visit nationalgeographic.com, call 1-877-873-6846, or write to the following address:
National Geographic Partners, LLC
1145 17th Street NW
Washington, DC 20036-4688 U.S.A.

For librarians and teachers: nationalgeographic.com/books/librarians-and-educators

More for kids from National Geographic: natgeokids.com

National Geographic Kids magazine inspires children to explore their world with fun yet educational articles on animals, science, nature, and more. Using fresh storytelling and amazing photography, *Nat Geo Kids* shows kids ages 6 to 14 the fascinating truth about the world—and why they should care. **natgeo.com/subscribe**

For rights or permissions inquiries, please contact National Geographic Books Subsidiary Rights: bookrights@natgeo.com

Illustrations by Oksana Drachkovska
Designed by Eva Absher-Schantz

Photographs integrated into the artist's illustrations provided by Shutterstock.
Author portrait by Lori Epstein; illustrator portrait courtesy of Oksana Drachkovska.

Hardcover ISBN: 978-1-4263-7372-5
Reinforced library binding ISBN: 978-1-4263-7510-1

The author would like to thank Oksana Drachkovska for her wonderful illustrations, along with art director Eva Absher-Schantz, photo editor Lori Epstein, cartographer Mike McNey, editor Marfé Ferguson Delano, and the rest of the team at National Geographic Kids Books.

Printed in China
23/RRDH/1